GETTING THE JOB DONE

GARBAGE COLLECTORS

Jill Sherman

PowerKiDS
press

New York

Published in 2020 by The Rosen Publishing Group, Inc.
29 East 21st Street, New York, NY 10010

First Edition

Editor: Greg Roza
Book Design: Reann Nye

Photo Credits: Cover Don Mason/Getty Images; p. 5 360b/Shutterstock.com; p. 6 InStock/ Image Source/Getty Images; p. 7 Library of Congress/Getty Images; p. 8 Peopleimages /E+/Getty Images; p. 9 Paolo Bona/Shutterstock.com; p. 11 Joseph Sohm/Shutterstock.com; p. 12 vchal/Shutterstock.com; p. 13 Digital Light Source/ Universal Images Group/Getty Images; p. 15 Don Mason/Getty Images; pp. 17, 22 Kzenon/Shutterstock.com; p. 19 Andrey_Popov/Shutterstock.com; p. 21 4x6/ iStock/Getty Images Plus/Getty Images.

Cataloging-in-Publication Data

Names: Sherman, Jill.
Title: Garbage collectors / Jill Sherman.
Description: New York : PowerKids Press, 2020. | Series: Getting the job done | Includes glossary and index.
Identifiers: ISBN 9781725300040 (pbk.) | ISBN 9781725300064 (library bound) | ISBN 9781725300057 (6pack)
Subjects: LCSH: Sanitation workers–Juvenile literature. | Refuse collectors–Juvenile literature. | Refuse collection–Juvenile literature. | Refuse and refuse disposal–Juvenile literature.
Classification: LCC HD8039.S257 S54 2020 | DDC 628.4′42′023–dc23

Manufactured in the United States of America

CPSIA Compliance Information: Batch #CSPK19. For Further Information contact Rosen Publishing, New York, New York at 1-800-237-9932.

CONTENTS

TAKING OUT THE GARBAGE

Every day, people throw away their garbage without thinking twice. Many things, such as pizza boxes and other takeout **containers**, are considered trash. In many places, people put their garbage bins on the curb to be collected every week. Once it's taken away, we often never think about our garbage again. Garbage collectors make this possible.

Garbage collectors, also called **sanitation** workers, play an important role in our communities. They help keep our communities and homes clean. Being a garbage collector means working long hours and doing hard, dirty work. Do you have what it takes to do this job?

Fascinating Career Facts

Garbage collectors keep us and Earth healthy. If trash piles up, the ground may absorb it, or soak it up. Garbage that the ground absorbs can pollute the land, attract pests, and cause sicknesses.

Garbage collectors dump bags and bins full of garbage into trucks every day. The trucks haul it to a **landfill** where it is buried.

OUR FILTHY PAST

For many years, people took care of their own garbage. It was buried, burned, and fed to farm animals. As cities got bigger, trash became a bigger problem. People tossed it onto the street and it piled up. The waste got into drinking water and made people sick.

Fascinating Career Facts

Garbage collectors are often referred to as "garbagemen." However, women are garbage collectors, too. In 2008, New York-City employed 7,000 garbage collectors and more than 200 of them were women.

Early garbage collectors cleaned up trash that gathered in the street.

In 1757, Benjamin Franklin started the first street cleaning service in America. Garbage collectors hauled waste out of cities on carts. Sometimes the garbage was burned. As **technology** improved, so did garbage collection. Over time, cities and towns everywhere began employing garbage collectors to help keep the streets clean.

7

A DIRTY JOB

Garbage collectors start their day early in the morning. Every day, they travel a different **route**. This way, they can cover the entire city or town during a week. Garbage collectors may visit 1,000 homes in a day. One person drives the garbage truck. Two other people ride on the back of the truck and pick up the garbage bins.

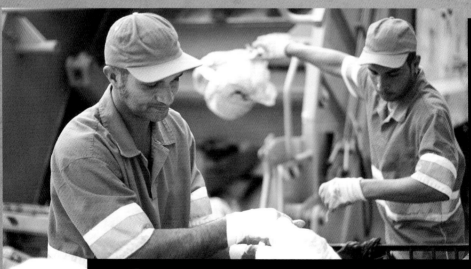

Fascinating Career Facts

The longer your garbage sits, the smellier it gets! Garbage collectors hardly notice how smelly garbage is because, after just a few minutes, their brain blocks it out.

Events such as festivals and food markets can leave city streets filled with trash. It's up to garbage collectors to clean up the mess!

Not everyone gets rid of their garbage the right way. Some people put large tree limbs or furniture out for collection. To take these things away, garbage collectors have to spend time breaking it into pieces. Other people overfill their garbage bags, which tear when lifted and create a big mess.

WASTE PROFESSIONALS

Garbage collectors are waste **professionals**. They know that not all kinds of waste should be mixed. To make garbage collectors' jobs easier, you should separate your waste by type. There are four types of waste: yard waste, construction waste, household waste, and **hazardous** waste.

Hazardous waste can't be collected with your regular waste on garbage day. Many cities hold hazardous waste drop-off days where you can bring things such as paint, oil, tires, and old electronics to a special place. From there, the hazardous waste is disposed of or recycled properly. Unfortunately, most cities only hold these drop-off days a few times a year.

Check your city's website to find out when the next household hazardous waste drop-off day is. It might be sooner than you think! >

WHERE DOES OUR GARBAGE GO?

Where your trash goes depends on where you live. Trash from many cities ends up in a landfill. Before it gets there, your garbage goes to a transfer station where it's offloaded, **compacted**, and loaded into bigger trucks. Then it'll be taken to a landfill.

The Fresh Kills Landfill on Staten Island, New York, was opened in 1948 and closed in 2001. This landfill was one of the biggest landfills in the world.

About 52 percent of the United States' garbage goes to landfills. Landfills are deep pits that are lined with clay and plastic sheets so hazardous chemicals don't leak into the ground. When the landfill gets full, it is covered with another sheet of plastic and dirt. The garbage decomposes, or breaks down, but this takes a long time.

SAFETY FIRST

Dealing with garbage is a dirty business. Garbage collectors must protect themselves from whatever is hiding inside our garbage bags and bins. If people put glass or hazardous waste in their garbage, it might hurt a garbage collector. To protect themselves, garbage collectors wear work gloves, long-sleeved shirts, and long pants. Being a garbage collector is also a noisy job. Garbage collectors wear earplugs or earmuffs to protect their hearing.

Garbage collectors work on busy roads. They wear **reflective** safety vests to help drivers see them. If you're behind a garbage truck, wait for the garbage collectors to wave to show you it's okay to pass the garbage truck.

Fascinating Career Facts

In 2017, 30 refuse and recyclable material collectors died as a result of work-related injuries. Make sure your parents drive safely near garbage collectors!

14

Reflective clothing shines bright in a car's headlights. This helps drivers see garbage collectors in all types of weather, no matter the time of day.

15

TRAINING AND EDUCATION

Many people can become a garbage collector. In most places, you must be at least 18 years old and have graduated from high school. Garbage collectors don't always need formal training. They are often paired up with an experienced worker and trained on the job. Over the course of their training, new garbage collectors will learn how to drive and operate the garbage truck, how to load dumpsters, and a number of other skills.

Garbage collectors who want to drive the garbage truck need to get their commercial driver's license, or CDL. In addition, some states require garbage collectors to have **hazmat** training.

Men and women can be garbage collectors. They just have to have a strong back, arms, and legs to lift heavy bags and bins.

>

Aufenthalt
zwischen den
Schränken
verboten

PAY AND BENEFITS

Garbage collectors in the United States make, on average, $36,160 per year, or about $17.38 per hour. In larger cities, garbage collectors are paid more. This is because garbage is collected more often in these areas to keep streets clean. Most garbage collectors work full time, or 40 hours a week. However, they often work **overtime**. Collecting garbage from city streets can't wait. Workers must complete their route, no matter how long it takes. This allows garbage collectors to earn even more.

Fascinating Career Facts

One person's trash is another's treasure! Garbage collectors can take home items they find in the garbage. People often throw away things that can be useful!

Some other benefits of being a garbage collector include making more money for working holidays, paid vacation, and health benefits. Some garbage collectors may even get a **pension**.

19

A GROWING INDUSTRY

According to the Bureau of Labor Statistics, there are about 115,130 garbage collectors working in the United States. Americans continue to throw away huge amounts of trash. This means the need for garbage collectors will continue to grow. This career path is expected to grow by around 7 percent a year until 2026.

New technology is also speeding up the job. Some trucks have special robotic arms that can lift garbage cans off the street. The trash is dumped into the truck without a collector having to touch it. This technology is making the job much safer and faster.

Being a garbage collector is hard on your body. It can also result in injuries such as sprains and broken bones. Some people have to stop working before the usual retirement age.

>

21

UP TO THE CHALLENGE?

What qualities make a good garbage collector? They should be physically fit to lift heavy objects all day. They must work long hours in all types of weather. Garbage collectors work through heat waves, rainstorms, and in freezing temperatures. People are constantly making trash. This means garbage collectors are constantly picking up trash. Garbage collectors have to be good at managing their time.

Garbage collectors must also be able to operate heavy machinery. Garbage trucks have a lot of moving parts. Garbage collectors need their trucks in good working condition to do their job. Are you up to the challenge of being a garbage collector?

GLOSSARY

compacted: Pressed tightly together.

container: Something into which other things can be put, such as for storage.

hazardous: Dangerous.

hazmat: A combination of the words "hazardous" and "material."

landfill: An area where waste is buried between layers of earth.

overtime: Time spent working that is more than one generally works in a day or a week.

pension: Money paid regularly to a person who has retired from work.

professional: A person who does a job that requires special education or skill.

reflective: Causing light to be thrown back.

route: A road or course of travel from one place to another.

sanitation: The process of keeping places free from dirt and disease.

technology: The way people do something and the tools they use.

INDEX

WEBSITES

Due to the changing nature of Internet links, PowerKids Press has developed an online list of websites related to the subject of this book. This site is updated regularly. Please use this link to access the list: www.powerkidslinks.com/GTJD/garbage